STONEWARE CREATIONS

DUNCAN
DESIGNERS

Valerie Ward
Michele Zulim

©1992 SCOTT PUBLICATIONS
30595 EIGHT MILE
LIVONIA, MI 48152-1798

ISBN # 0-916809-57-9
PRINTED IN USA
No. 3232-9-92

DESIGN
Connie Carley

PHOTOGRAPHY
Lorrie Messina

COVER PHOTO
Larry Krauter

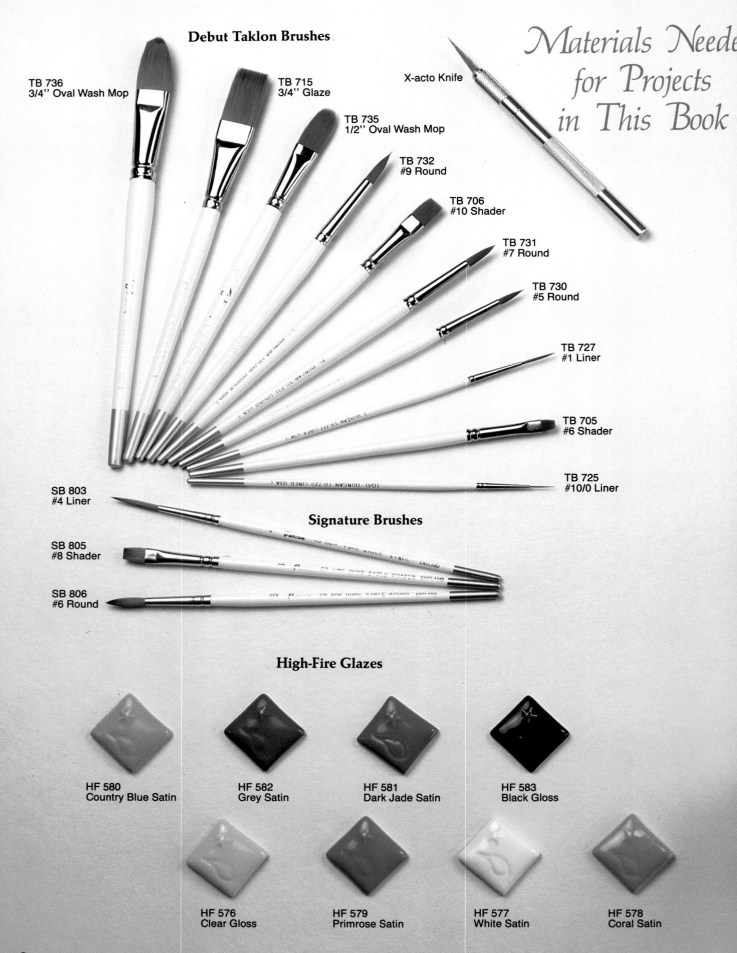

Debut Taklon Brushes

TB 736
3/4'' Oval Wash Mop

TB 715
3/4'' Glaze

TB 735
1/2'' Oval Wash Mop

TB 732
#9 Round

TB 706
#10 Shader

TB 731
#7 Round

TB 730
#5 Round

TB 727
#1 Liner

TB 705
#6 Shader

TB 725
#10/0 Liner

X-acto Knife

Signature Brushes

SB 803
#4 Liner

SB 805
#8 Shader

SB 806
#6 Round

High-Fire Glazes

HF 580
Country Blue Satin

HF 582
Grey Satin

HF 581
Dark Jade Satin

HF 583
Black Gloss

HF 576
Clear Gloss

HF 579
Primrose Satin

HF 577
White Satin

HF 578
Coral Satin

SW 520
Light Taupe Stoneware Tint

SW 523
Blush Beige Stoneware Tint

SW 522
Wedgwood Blue Stoneware Tint

Stoneware Slip and Stoneware Tints

SW 510
Cashmere Stoneware Slip

SW 521
Grey Stoneware Tint

SW 524
Mocha Stoneware Tint

TL 401
Cleanup

TL 411
Stylus

TL 407
Sgraffito-Duster

Tools

Large Sea Wool Sponge

TL 415
Replacement Sponge

TL 406
Lace Draper

Banding Wheel

Rubber-Scrubber

3

Introduction

Stoneware Creations is a technique book featuring Duncan products, molds, colors, stoneware slip, Stoneware Tints and High-Fire Glazes.

For information on how to mix slip and cast molds, Duncan offers a *Stoneware Information Guide.*

The *Duncan Color Selection Guide* presents glaze and underglaze colors recommended for stoneware decoration and also has a complete listing of all nontoxic glazes that can be used on stoneware and shows the color results.

For information on these products and guides, available molds, and seminars, contact your Duncan supplier or Duncan Enterprises, 5673 E. Shields Ave., Fresno, CA 93727.

Introducing Stoneware

It's simple, it's elegant, it's distinctively different!

You've probably noticed a turn to stoneware in the dinnerware, serving pieces and homewares currently offered by department stores and gift shops.

It's possible for ceramists to enjoy the excitement of a new dimension of hobby ceramics with Duncan stoneware products. For more detailed information on how you can use these products, please turn to pages 6-7 of this book.

Duncan stoneware products are nontoxic and dinnerware safe. After being fired to cone 6, they are vitreous (waterproof). Stoneware items are safe for use in conventional and microwave ovens and can be washed in an electric dishwasher. Above all else, Duncan Stoneware is highly chip-resistant.

There are 12 stoneware decorating projects in this book in four different categories: French Country, Simple Pleasures, Southwest and Contemporary. There are three projects in each category: beginner, intermediate and advanced.

Whatever your level of expertise, you'll find these projects clearly labeled for your convenience. Please do not feel, however, that you are restricted to whatever level you believe you are. If you are a beginner and consider yourself so, you may still want to stretch your decorating skills by trying a project at the intermediate level. If you're a ceramist with intermediate skills, you can reach for an advanced project. And for those of you who consider yourselves advanced ceramists, you may want to decorate some of the beginner and intermediate projects simply because they are beautiful examples of what stoneware can be.

About the Authors and Their Aims:

Michele Zulim and Valerie Ward are two of the talented ceramics artists and designers who create projects to illustrate the Duncan products that appear in Duncan's catalogs, brochures, color sheets and more. In addition, their work has been published in various ceramics magazines.

Their lifelong interest in art has been encouraged and stimulated by college classes and seminars covering all forms of art work, in such diverse media as pottery, oils, pastels, and pen-and-ink drawings.

Michele and Valerie are inspired by the sheer joy of color and the many different ceramic products that expand the palette of colors and the range of finishes they are able to use for their creations.

In this book, Michele and Valerie have focused on stoneware and the glazes and underglazes that can be used for high-fire ware. They have also taken advantage of the color of the stoneware body, and some projects feature tinted stoneware slip. The result is a book designed to share the pleasures of stoneware decorating with everyone.

Table of Contents

About Stoneware

Stoneware Slip

As a ceramics hobbyist, the thing that will interest you most about Duncan Stoneware Slip is that it enables your supplier to provide you with stoneware greenware cast with the highest quality slip on the market.

If, however, you decide that you would like to try casting your own stoneware pieces, your supplier offers SW 510 Cashmere Stoneware Slip in 1-gallon jars and a great selection of molds.

Stoneware Tints

As you noticed, page 3 of this book displays all the Stoneware Tints that can be used to change the color of the basic Cashmere Stoneware Slip. Once again, you will not actually use the Stoneware Tints unless you cast your own molds.

What Stoneware Tints offer ceramics hobbyists is the option of ordering stoneware greenware in different colors. You can tell your supplier what Stoneware Tint you want—you can even be creative and make up your own colors by ordering Cashmere Stoneware Slip tinted with two Stoneware Tint colors.

The basic formula for tinting Stoneware Slip calls for 4 ozs. of Stoneware Tint added to 1 gallon of Cashmere Stoneware Slip. Variations of color can be achieved. This formula can be varied by adding 1 oz. of one Stoneware Tint and 3 ozs. of another Tint, or to deepen add 8 ozs. of a Stoneware Tint.

Subtle colorations can be created by adding only 1 or 2 ozs. of Stoneware Tint to a gallon of slip.

For truly creative stoneware decorating, make yourself familiar with the various Stoneware Tint colors so you can order distinctively different stoneware greenware from your supplier.

The projects in this book that are done on tinted stoneware are called out with the amount and name of the Stoneware Tint added to each gallon of Cashmere Stoneware Slip.

Cleaning Stoneware

This is the most important information you need for successful and beautiful stoneware decorating. Just as with low-fire ceramic greenware, careful attention to proper greenware preparation is all important for finely finished stoneware.

Greenware comes with seam lines created where the halves of the mold join together. Preparing or cleaning the greenware are the terms used for removing these seam lines and other small imperfections from the greenware before it is decorated.

Here are some important points about cleaning stoneware:

- *Clean only one color of stoneware at a time. Do not mix the dust of different stoneware colors when cleaning. One color could adhere to another, causing discoloration. Also, do not allow low-fire earthenware dust to adhere to the ware's surface. Earthenware dust will become shiny at high-fire temperatures.*

- For best results, the stoneware greenware should be bone-dry. If it is damp, you could score the ware while removing the seam line. To remove the seam line, use a TL 401 cleanup tool or an X-acto knife with a sharp blade. Stoneware is abrasive and will dull the blade, so change the blade as needed. Be careful. Stoneware greenware is as fragile as regular earthenware greenware but not as brittle as porcelain greenware.

- The ware can also be sanded with a 100 grit rubber scrubber. Try not to over clean or make deep scratches in the ware's surface.

- Once the ware is cleaned to your satisfaction, use a dampened sponge to go over the entire piece of greenware. Be sure to work out any scratches and remaining blemishes. Rinse the sponge often and do not leave a heavy residue of clay buildup. Change the water in your bowl often. Be careful not to leave the imprint of the wet sponge on the ware's surface as the imprint could show up after firing. A soft glaze brush dampened with water can be worked over the ware as well.

- Let the ware dry 24 hours before firing to prevent pieces from cracking or exploding.

Firing Stoneware

If you do not own a kiln and let your supplier fire your pieces, you can skip this section.

If you do own a kiln and want to fire your decorated stoneware, make sure your kiln has at least a cone 6 rating or higher.

Prepare the kiln in the same way as for a low-fire firing. Place kiln wash on the sensing rod, cone supports and the top side of the kiln shelves. The peephole plugs should be left in if the kiln lid has a vent hole. If your kiln does not have a lid vent hole, leave the top peephole plug out during the entire firing.

If your kiln has never had a high-fire break-in firing, do this before actually firing a load of stoneware.

High fire the kiln once with just kiln shelves and witness cones to ensure proper high-fire results. Be sure to keep track of the length of the firing time; stoneware will take longer to fire. A longer time span is necessary for proper high-fire results.

Fire the kiln two hours on LOW, then two hours on MEDIUM, and then on HI-FIRE for a long, slow firing cycle. If you have an automatic kiln, the programmed automatic cycle is suitable for stoneware.

Stoneware pieces cannot be stilted. Stilts will bend at high temperatures and could pierce and distort the ware. When firing pieces with lids, the two pieces must be fired together to prevent warpage and ensure proper fit. All pieces should be fired in their normal resting or sitting position.

When firing pieces with lids or covers, the glazed areas cannot touch each other. Therefore, do not glaze or underglaze any part of the items that will come in contact with one another.

NOTE: Apply a mixture of 4 parts SY 547 Wax Resist and 1 part alumina hydrate to the contact areas of lids and containers. This mixture helps prevent pieces from fusing together in the high firing.

The kiln should not be overly packed with ware. High firing demands plenty of heat and air circulation.

When high firing glazed and unglazed items, place the glazed ware on one shelf and the unglazed ware on another. The glaze could flash a soft glossy sheen onto the unglazed ware. Additionally, be sure to fire like color values on the same shelf. Do not fire a dark-glazed item next to a light-glazed item. Some discoloration could take place on the light-colored ware.

Unglazed handles for mugs, cups, tureens, etc. may need to be supported in firing by placing a post with kiln wash on it next to the handle. This may help retain the ware's shape during the firing.

Do not cool the kiln rapidly and do not open the kiln while it is still hot or warm. Stoneware is subject to cracking (thermal shock) when cooled too rapidly. As with low-fire clays, do not open the kiln until it is *cool to the touch.*

Kiln wash that adheres to the bottom of the ware can be sanded off with a 100 grit rubber-scrubber. If a stoneware high-fire load is underfired, the pieces can be refired to witness cone 6 without adverse effects. Colored clays will be lighter in tone if underfired.

If stoneware is overfired, the item could slump or sag and turn slightly shiny. Also, the colored clays could darken and the surface of the slip could bubble. However, Duncan stoneware can be fired as high as cone 10.

NOTE: Stoneware shrinks 12-13% when fired to cone 6.

Decorating Stoneware

Because stoneware is most often used for kitchenware, serving pieces and dinnerware, *nontoxic, dinnerware-safe glazes and underglazes for decorating these pieces must be used. ALL THE COLORS USED IN THIS BOOK ARE NONTOXIC AND DINNERWARE SAFE.*

If you want to use a glaze or underglaze not included in the guide, always make a small fired test before proceeding with your project.

General Decorating

Duncan's Stoneware is a one-fire clay body. That means that all decorating can be done on the greenware including the glazing. The basic application of color products is as follows: 1) clean greenware; 2) decorate the ware with your choice of underglazes and let dry; 3) if desired, apply appropriate glaze (HF 576 Clear Gloss over underglaze decoration); 4) fire to witness cone 6.

High-Fire Glazes

Duncan's High-Fire glazes have been developed solely for use on stoneware and porcelain. These glazes are designed to mature at witness cone 6 and can be used only on high-fire clay bodies. They will not work at lower temperatures. High-Fire glazes are nontoxic lead-free glazes that are dinnerware safe.

High-Fire glazes are overglaze compatible.

Low-Fire Glazes

The products are applied in the usual manner with 3-coat coverage. However, all glaze products should be applied to greenware or cone 018-016 bisque. Be sure to apply these products to thoroughly dampened ware and, if the glaze is thick, thin with water or Thin 'n Shade to achieve normal (cream-like) brushing consistency. The usual 3-coat application will be necessary to achieve proper coverage on the stoneware body.

Premixed E-Z Stroke® Translucent Underglazes

These translucent underglazes should be used in the same manner on stoneware as on earthenware. Depending upon the desired effect, cream, light-cream and milk (wash) consistencies are used. The colors are normally applied to greenware, but antiquing wash can be applied to cone 018-016 bisque.

E-Z Stroke colors will be more opaque than translucent if left unglazed.

Translucent properties will develop after a final glaze has been applied and fired to witness cone 6.

Design-Coat® Versatile Underglazes & Cover-Coat® Opaque Underglazes

These colors can be applied directly to stoneware greenware or to witness cone 018-016 bisque. Keep the application smooth as 3 coats are applied. Cover-Coats remain opaque but some changes could occur due to the high firing.

If a glaze finish over the Cover-Coat is desired, let the decorated ware dry thoroughly and apply an appropriate nontoxic transparent glaze that can be high fired over the ware. Use a soft glaze brush and be careful not to move or smear the previously applied Cover-Coat design.

E-Z Strokes can also be applied over the Cover-Coat for further decoration and design work. However, when glazing, again be very careful not to disturb the colors.

Decorating Tinted Stoneware

Items cast with tinted stoneware slip can be finished quickly and beautifully by applying HF 576 Clear Gloss to the inside and firing the ware to cone 6. For further accents, decorate glazed areas with OG 801 Bright Gold or OG 802 White Gold Overglaze and fire to cone 019. Keep in mind that these overglazes are dinnerware safe but *not* dishwasher safe. Overglaze-decorated pieces will need to be washed by hand.

Ceramics Terms in This Book

Antiquing Easy and very attractive color effects can be achieved by applying a color to the surface of the ware and then wiping it back with a dampened sponge, leaving the antiquing color in creviced areas. The ware must be allowed to dry thoroughly before proceeding with the decorating technique. For best results, use this technique on cone 018-016 soft fired ware.

Butting This is a term used to describe the placement of two or more glazes in close proximity on the same piece. The second glaze is applied so that it comes within the width of a pencil-point line of the first glaze but does not touch it. If the glazes accidentally touch, the area is scraped clean with the Cleanup tool, then retouched. The butting technique prevents glazes from flowing together during firing.

Comma Strokes These are brush-strokes shaped like a comma. Comma strokes can be made in either direction, forward or backward. They are very useful in creating floral and leaf designs. The motion of the brush is press, pull and lift.

Conditioning Because Mask 'n Peel is a water-based emulsion that is hard to remove from unprotected brushes, always dampen the brush thoroughly with Hand and Brush Cleaner and squeeze out the excess before loading the conditioned brush with Mask 'n Peel. Clean the brush in Hand and Brush Cleaner and rinse in warm water immediately after the Mask 'n Peel is applied.

Consistency This refers to the degree of color thickness or solidity especially of a liquid or soft mixture. When a certain consistency is specified, add a little water at a time to the color until the desired consistency is achieved.

Damp-Sponge Using a sponge dampened with water to remove clay dust from greenware or ware fired to cone 018-016 bisque.

Dots A very easy form of decorating obtained by dipping the end of a brush handle or the Stylus into color spread on a palette and then lightly stamping it onto the ware. Dots descending in size (often called "descending dots") are achieved by continuing to dot without reloading the tool. As the color is used, the dots become smaller.

Floated Strokes These brush-strokes are achieved by dipping a shader brush in water and then touching each side of the brush once to a paper towel to remove excess water. The brush is then side loaded in color and touched once or twice to the palette to work the color through the brush hairs, allowing the color to "float." The loaded side of the brush is then placed toward the outside or the inside as desired to create floated-stroke shading. The realistic shading achieved by this method is nothing short of amazing.

Marking Guidelines with a Banding Wheel This technique uses a banding wheel, which is a hand-operated turntable. To successfully use the banding wheel, follow these steps. Place a plastic bag filled with rice inside the ware. The rice is small enough so that it will evenly weight the ware to prevent it from flying off the turntable. Judging by eye, place the ware in the center of the turntable. Now use a soft lead pencil to mark a line on the ware as you rotate the turntable. If the pencil line is even, the ware is properly centered. If, however, the pencil line skips, pull the ware slightly toward you where the skip occurred and try the process over again until the penciled line is continuous. The banding wheel is a useful tool for marking off bands for design work. It is also often employed for applying color directly to the ware.

Palette A surface used to spread paint on. This can be a professional ceramics artist's glazed palette (purchased from your supplier or an art shop) or a glazed saucer or flat dish. Palette paper will also work well.

Rolling Glaze Some ware, such as pitchers and vases, may be too deep for brush application of glaze. The answer here is to roll glaze inside the piece. Use a stir stick and paper cup to mix glaze with water to specified consistency (light cream for 3-coat glazes; milk for 2-coat glazes). Pour the glaze into the ware and roll around until the inside is completely coated. Return the excess glaze to the paper cup. Remove any drips from the outside of the ware with a water-dampened sponge.

Sgraffito Sgraffito (scratching) is a term that comes to us from Italian. It is done much the same as incising except that the design is done by gently scratching through applied color to reveal the stoneware body beneath it.

Sketch Sometimes it is possible to sketch a design on the ware without using a pattern. To do this, use a soft lead pencil to lightly sketch guidelines or a design on the greenware, being careful not to dent the ware.

Sponging This easy technique employs a slightly dampened sponge to apply color to the ware. The color is spread on a palette and the sponge is used to pick up the color to be applied. The effects vary, depending on whether the sponge used has large or fine pores.

French Country Cottage Pitcher

**DM-1324 Cottage Pitcher
DM-1325 Handle for DM-1324
Cast with 1 gal. SW 510
Cashmere Stoneware Slip
mixed with 2 4-oz. jars of
SW 522 Wedgwood Blue
Stoneware Tint**

MATERIALS
HF 577 White Satin
TB 715 3/4'' Glaze
TL 401 Cleanup or X-acto
  Knife
TL 415 Replacement Sponge
  or Large Sea Wool Sponge
Paper Cup
Stir Stick
Rubber-Scrubber

Step 1 — Using the cleanup tool, carefully clean the seam lines and lip around the pitcher.

Step 2 — Damp-sponge the outside of the pitcher with a large sponge to remove any dust.

Step 3 — Soft fire the ware to cone 018. Note: This piece can be put in with any overglaze cone 018 firing to save space and energy.

Step 4 — Using a paper cup and stir stick, thin White Satin with water to a light cream consistency. Roll the thinned glaze inside the pitcher, then pour excess glaze from the pitcher back into the paper cup. Wipe away any drips from the outside with a dampened sponge.

Step 5 — Use the glaze brush to apply 1 heavy coat of White Satin to the basket-weave area of the pitcher.

Step 6 — Wipe back glaze with a large sponge to create an antiqued effect, being careful not to wipe away too much detail. Be sure no glaze is on the bottom of the pitcher.

Step 7 — Using the glaze brush, carefully apply 3 flowing coats of undiluted White Satin to the upper lip area of the pitcher, avoiding the decorated basket-weave area and the handle.

Step 8 — Using a sponge, thoroughly dampen the ware around the outside lip and the entire inside of the pitcher.

Step 9 — Fire to cone 6.

Step 10 — Use a rubber-scrubber to smooth the undecorated areas of the fired stoneware surface.

French Country Designer 10" Dinner Plate

**DM-775 Designer 10"
Dinner Plate
Cast with SW 510 Stoneware Cashmere Slip**
(Note: For a complete Designer Dinnerware Set, you'll need stoneware greenware cast from DM-776 Salad Plate, DM-777 Cup, DM-778 Saucer, DM-779 Bowl, DM-780 Sugar Bowl and DM-781 Creamer.)

MATERIALS
CC 112 Light Flesh
CC 135 Lake Blue
CC 161 Blue Green
CC 163 Danish Blue
CC 176 Pueblo Purple
HF 576 Clear Gloss
TB 730 #5 Round
TB 731 #7 Round
TB 736 3/4" Oval Wash Mop
TL 401 Cleanup or X-acto
 Knife
TL 411 Stylus
TL 415 Replacement Sponge
 or Large Sea Wool Sponge
Ruler
Soft Lead Pencil
Banding Wheel
Rubber-Scrubber

Step 1 — Using the cleanup tool, carefully prepare the greenware. Thoroughly damp-sponge the plate with a large sponge.

Step 2 — With a ruler, carefully mark 1"-wide stripes with 1/2" between each stripe. Keep the stripes as straight as possible.

Step 3 — Center the plate on a banding wheel. Place a plastic bag filled with rice on top of the plate. Judging by eye, place the ware in the center of the turntable. Now use a soft lead pencil to mark a line on the edge of the plate as you rotate the turntable. If the pencil line is even, the ware is properly centered. If, however, the pencil line skips, pull the ware slightly toward you where the skip occurred and try the process over again until the penciled line is continuous. Use the banding wheel to mark a 1/4"-wide band on the flat inner area of the plate and another 1/4"-wide band on the outer rim of the plate. Remove bag of rice.

Step 4 — Use the #7 round brush to apply 3 smooth, even coats of Blue Green to the 1"-wide stripes.

Step 5 — Gently sketch a bow-and-streamer design around the border of the plate, leaving approximately 3 1/2" open at the bottom of the plate.

Step 6 — Using either the #5 or #7 round brush, apply 3 smooth, even coats of Lake Blue to the light areas of the bow and streamers. Apply 3 smooth, even coats of Danish Blue to the dark and shaded areas of the bow design, overlapping the Lake Blue areas if necessary.

Step 7 — Using Light Flesh and the #5 round brush, paint in heart shapes onto the Blue Green stripes; apply 2 additional coats of Light Flesh to each heart.

Step 8 — Using the stylus, with 2 coats of Pueblo Purple, create dots along the edges of the Blue Green stripes.

Step 9 — Apply 2 flowing coats of Clear Gloss glaze to the center of the plate, using the oval wash mop brush. Make sure there is no glaze on the back of the plate.

Step 10 — Fire to cone 6.

Step 11 — Use a rubber-scrubber to smooth the undecorated areas of the fired stoneware surface.

French Country Country Cupboard Bowl

DM-604C Country Cupboard Bowl

Cast with 1 gal. SW 510 Cashmere Stoneware Slip mixed with 4 oz. SW 520 Light Taupe Stoneware Tint

MATERIALS
EZ 023 Midnight Blue
EZ 024 Royal Blue Green
EZ 026 Yellow Orange
EZ 031 Light Blue
EZ 034 Orange
EZ 043 Mint Julep
CC 101 Arctic White
CC 163 Danish Blue
RI 563 Steel Blue
FD 251 Steel Blue
FD 258 Pure White
FD 262 Deep Jade
TB 706 No. 10 Shader
TB 715 ³/₄'' Glaze
TB 725 #10/0 Liner
TB 727 #1 Liner
TB 730 #5 Round
TB 731 #7 Round
TL 401 Cleanup or X-acto Knife
TL 411 Stylus
TL 415 Replacement Sponge or Large Sea Wool Sponge
Banding Wheel
Soft Lead Pencil
Palette
Rubber-Scrubber

Step 1 — Using the cleanup tool, carefully prepare the greenware. Thoroughly damp-sponge the entire bowl.

Step 2 — Center the bowl on a banding wheel. Mark guidelines for bands as follows: first line ¹/₂'' down from glaze line; second, ¹/₄'' down; third, 1¹/₂'' down; and fourth, ¹/₄'' down.

Step 3 — Use the glaze brush to apply 3 flowing coats of Steel Blue River Rock glaze inside the bowl and ¹/₂'' down the outer lip.

Step 4 — Apply 3 smooth, even coats of Arctic White to the center band, using the glaze brush.

Step 5 — Using the #7 round brush, apply 3 smooth, even coats of Danish Blue to the narrow bands on each side of the white band.

Step 6 — Gently sketch a wavy line in the white band as a guide for the flowers.

Step 7 — Place a small amount of each E-Z Stroke color on separate areas of a palette. If needed, thin colors to a cream consistency.

Step 8 — Load the #5 round brush in Orange and tip the brush in Yellow Orange. Press two strokes side by side to create the centers of the five-petaled flowers.

Step 9 — Load the #5 round brush in Light Blue and press two strokes side by side to create petals for the flowers.

Step 10 — Using the #10/0 liner brush, detail the flowers with Midnight Blue with broken hit-and-miss outlines around the petals and the center. Also pull out two to three fine vein lines from the center of each petal.

Step 11 — Using the stylus, add Midnight Blue dots to the lower half of each five-petaled flower.

Step 12 — Load the #5 round brush in Light Blue and tip the brush in Midnight Blue. Use press, pull and lift comma strokes together to create three-petaled flowers.

Step 13 — Using the shader brush, side load in Light Blue and Midnight Blue. With the Light Blue to the outside, wiggle the brush back and forth on its chisel edge to create the upper half circle of each fan flower, to make a rippled fan stroke.

Step 14 — Again using the shader brush, side load in Midnight Blue and Royal Blue Green. With Royal Blue Green to the bottom, wiggle the brush back and forth on its chisel edge to create the bottom half of each fan flower.

Step 15 — Using the stylus, add Midnight Blue dots along the outer tips of the fan flowers.

Step 16 — Add wavy stems and sepals with Royal Blue Green, using the #1 liner brush.

Step 17 — Using the #5 round brush, load in Royal Blue Green and tip in Mint Julep. Create long press, pull and lift leaves for the fan flowers, comma stroke heart-shaped leaves for the three-petaled flowers, and single comma stroke leaves for five-petaled flowers.

Step 18 — Using the #10/0 and #1 liner brushes as needed, add swirls and tendrils of Royal Blue Green as desired throughout the flower design.

Step 19 — Add Deep Jade dots to the base of the three-petaled flowers and three dots of Pure White to the top of the three-petaled flowers.

Step 20 — Using Steel Blue French Dimensions, add clusters of dots randomly throughout the design as desired.

Step 21 — Fire to cone 6.

Step 22 — Use a rubber-scrubber to smooth the undecorated areas of the fired stoneware surface.

Simple Pleasures Loaf Pan

DM-1503 Loaf Pan
Cast with SW 510 Cashmere Stoneware Slip

MATERIALS
EZ 011 Sienna Brown
EZ 038 Medium Mahogany
RI 560 White
SY 548 Mask 'n Peel
AS 952 Hand and Brush
  Cleaner
TB 715 ³/₄'' Glaze
TB 730 #5 Round
TL 401 Cleanup or X-acto
  Knife
TL 407 Sgraffito-Duster
TL 415 Replacement Sponge
  or Large Sea Wool Sponge
Graphite Paper or Clay
  Carbon
Soft Lead Pencil
Palette
Rubber-Scrubber

Step 1 — Using the cleanup tool, carefully prepare the greenware. Thoroughly damp-sponge the loaf pan with a large sponge.

Step 2 — Using graphite paper, gently transfer the pattern onto the sides and ends of the loaf pan.

Step 3 — Use the Sgraffito-Duster to incise designs into the loaf pan. In areas where two lines intersect, pull the tool away from a point on each side of the previously incised line. Remove dust with the brush end of the tool. Use a glaze brush to remove any remaining dust and lightly damp-sponge the ware.

Step 4 — Fire to cone 018.

Step 5 — Place a small amount of each E-Z Stroke color on separate areas of a palette. If needed, thin the colors with water to a cream consistency. Working with one color at a time, use the glaze brush to apply Sienna Brown and Medium Mahogany here and there over the wheat designs. Allow to dry.

Step 6 — Remove excess color from the design areas with a dampened sponge, leaving colors in incised areas. Let dry.

Step 7 — Condition the round brush with Hand and Brush Cleaner. Use the conditioned brush to carefully apply Mask 'n Peel to the outer rim of the loaf pan. Allow to dry.

Step 8 — Damp-sponge the inside of the loaf pan. Use the glaze brush to apply 3 flowing coats of White to the inside and top rim of the loaf pan. Remove Mask 'n Peel.

Step 9 — Fire to cone 6.

Step 10 — Use a rubber-scrubber to smooth the undecorated areas of the fired stoneware surface.

PATTERN ON PAGE 37

Simple Pleasures Soup Tureen

DM-1507 Soup Tureen
DM-1508 Handles for DM-1507
DM-1509 Lid for DM-1507 Cast with 1 gal. SW 510 Cashmere Stoneware Slip mixed with 4 oz. SW 523 Blush Beige Stoneware Tint

MATERIALS
EZ 011 Sienna Brown
EZ 012 Cobalt Jet Black
EZ 013 White
EZ 028 Leaf Green
EZ 033 Ivy Green
EZ 038 Medium Mahogany
HF 577 White Satin
SY 548 Mask 'n Peel
TB 725 #10/0 Liner
TB 730 #5 Round
TL 401 Cleanup or X-acto
  Knife
TL 415 Replacement Sponge
  or Large Sea Wool Sponge
Graphite Paper or Clay
  Carbon
Soft Lead Pencil
Paper Cup
Stir Stick
Palette
Stiff Brush
Rubber-Scrubber

Step 1 — Using the cleanup tool, carefully prepare the greenware. Thoroughly damp-sponge the tureen and lid with a large sponge.

Step 2 — Gently transfer patterns onto the tureen and lid with graphite paper.

Step 3 — Condition the Round brush with the Hand and Brush Cleaner. Use the conditioned brush to apply Mask 'n Peel to the inner rim of the lid and to the rim and top ³/₄″ inside the tureen. Allow to dry.

Step 4 — Use a large sponge to dampen the inside of the tureen and lid with water. Using a paper cup

and stir stick, thin White Satin with water to a light cream consistency. Roll the thinned glaze inside the tureen and lid, then pour excess glaze back into the paper cup. Wipe away any drips from outside areas with a dampened sponge. Remove Mask 'n Peel.

Step 5 — Apply 3 flowing coats of undiluted White Satin glaze to the handles, using the round brush.

Step 6 — Place a small amount of each E-Z Stroke color on separate areas of a palette. If needed, thin the colors to a cream consistency.

Step 7 — Use the round brush to apply the following colors to designated areas:
Ivy Green — Borders of leaves and some strokes from center of leaves to outer edge.
Leaf Green — Some random strokes from center of leaves to outer edge.
Sienna Brown — Here and there on leaves.
White — Here and there on leaves.

Step 8 — Use the liner brush to create the stems, leaf outlines and tendrils with the following randomly applied colors: Medium Mahogany, Ivy Green and Cobalt Jet Black.

Step 9 — Mix four parts Wax Resist and one part alumina hydrate. Use the #5 round brush to apply the mixture to contact areas of the tureen and lid.

Step 10 — With the lid in place on the tureen, fire to cone 6.

Step 11 — Remove the protective mixture from the tureen and lid with a stiff bristle brush.

Step 12 — Use a rubber-scrubber to smooth the undecorated areas of the fired stoneware surface.

PATTERN ON PAGE 35

Simple Pleasures Wine Cooler

DM-1500 Wine Cooler Cast with SW 510 Cashmere Stoneware Slip

MATERIALS
EZ 004 Willow Yellow
EZ 007 Royal Purple
EZ 011 Sienna Brown
EZ 012 Cobalt Jet Black
EZ 026 Yellow Orange
EZ 028 Leaf Green
EZ 032 Peacock Green
EZ 038 Medium Mahogany
CC 101 Arctic White
CC 104 Princess Yellow
TB 715 ³/₄'' Glaze
TB 725 #10/0 Liner
TB 730 #5 Round
TL 401 Cleanup or X-acto
  Knife
TL 407 Sgraffito-Duster
TL 415 Replacement Sponge
  or Large Sea Wool Sponge
Graphite Paper or Clay
  Carbon
Soft Lead Pencil
Palette
Rubber-Scrubber

Step 1 — Using cleanup tool, carefully prepare greenware. Thoroughly damp-sponge the entire wine cooler.

Step 2 — Using the glaze brush, apply 3 smooth, even coats of Arctic White to the outside of the dampened ware. Allow to dry.

Step 3 — Transfer the pattern onto the wine cooler with graphite paper.

Step 4 — Apply 3 smooth, even coats of Princess Yellow to the sunflower petals with the round brush.

Step 5 — Place a small amount of each E-Z Stroke color on separate areas of a palette. If needed, thin the colors to a cream consistency.

Step 6 — Apply the following E-Z Stroke colors to designated areas with the round brush unless otherwise noted:
Willow Yellow—Several strokes from base to tip of each petal.
Yellow Orange—Several strokes from base to tip of each petal and sunflower centers.
Sienna Brown—Centers of flowers, some random strokes and petals, leaves and stems for shading. (Use the liner brush for small details.)
Medium Mahogany—Around edges of centers and several strokes in centers.
Leaf Green—Stems and leaves.
Peacock Green—Randomly on stems and leaves.
Royal Purple—Some shading around centers. (Make a wash and shade petals with the liner brush.)
Cobalt Jet Black—Use the liner brush to randomly outline petals, leaves and stems.

Step 7 — Using the sgraffito-duster, sgraffito around the petals, leaves and stems, and add detailing to the centers of the flowers. Use the brush end of the tool to remove dust.

Step 8 — Fire to cone 6.

Step 9 — Use a rubber-scrubber to smooth the undecorated areas of the fired stoneware surface.

Note: The wine cooler should be placed in the freezer two hours before using with chilled wine bottle or other bottled beverage.

PATTERN ON PAGE 36

Southwest Chip & Dip Bowl

**DM-1057 Chip & Dip Bowl
Cast with 1 gal. SW 510
Cashmere Stoneware Slip
mixed with 4 oz. SW 524
Mocha Stoneware Tint**

Materials
EZ 053 Hacienda Jade
EZ 056 Brick Red
EZ 057 Coral Red
EZ 058 Poppy Orange
HF 576 Clear Gloss
HF 581 Dark Jade Satin
TB 730 #5 Round
TB 735 1/2'' Oval Wash Mop
TL 401 Cleanup or X-acto
  Knife
TL 407 Sgraffito-Duster
TL 415 Replacement Sponge
  or Large Sea Wool Sponge
Palette
Rubber-Scrubber

Step 1 — Using the cleanup tool, carefully prepare the greenware. Thoroughly damp-sponge the bowl with a large sponge.

Step 2 — Place a small amount of each E-Z Stroke color on separate areas of a palette. If needed, thin the colors to a cream consistency.

Step 3 — Lightly sketch a pepper design on the chip area of the bowl.

Step 4 — Load the oval wash mop in Coral Red and tip in Poppy Orange. Create peppers in the chip area of the bowl by pressing the brush down at the tip of the pepper and wiggling it back and forth to create a pepper shape. Alternate loading and tipping the colors with each other and with Brick Red to create differently colored peppers, being careful that the E-Z Strokes are not too thickly applied.

Step 5 — Using the round brush, create the pepper caps and stems with Hacienda Jade. Allow to dry.

Step 6 — Using the sgraffito-duster, gently carve outlines around the peppers and caps, and add random highlight lines on the peppers. Use the brush end of the tool to remove dust and particles.

Step 7 — Apply 3 flowing coats of Dark Jade Satin to the inner cup and outer rim with the oval wash mop brush.

Step 8 — Use the oval wash mop brush to apply 2 flowing coats of Clear Gloss to the chip area.

Step 9 — Fire to cone 6.

Step 10 — Use a rubber-scrubber to smooth the undecorated areas of the fired stoneware surface.

Southwest Pueblo Village Candle Holder

DM-1376 Pueblo Village Candle Holder

Cast with SW 510 Cashmere Stoneware Slip

MATERIALS
EZ 007 Royal Purple
EZ 011 Sienna Brown
EZ 019 Smoke Grey
EZ 034 Orange
EZ 038 Medium Mahogany
EZ 049 Mojave Sand
EZ 051 Santa Fe Sunset
HF 583 Black Gloss
TB 705 #6 Shader
TB 727 #1 Liner
TB 730 #5 Round
TB 735 1/2" Oval Wash Mop
TL 401 Cleanup
TL 406 Lace Draper
X-acto Knife
Small Silk Sponge
Palette
Paper Towels
Toothpicks
Rubber-Scrubber

Step 1 — Soon after removing the candle holder from the mold, use the lace draper to pierce holes for stars and an X-acto knife to cut out the moon and some windows. (If using studio greenware, order with cuts made.)

Step 2 — Using the cleanup tool, carefully prepare the greenware. Damp-sponge the candle holder and insert with a small silk sponge.

Step 3 — Soft fire to cone 018.

Step 4 — Place a small amount of each E-Z Stroke color on separate areas of a palette. If needed, thin the colors to a cream consistency.

Step 5 — Using the shader and the round brushes as needed, apply Santa Fe Sunset to the mountains, being careful not to get color on the pueblos.

Step 6 — Shade the bottom edges of the mountains with Smoke Grey, pulling the shader brush upward toward the sky.

Step 7 — Repeat Step 4 with Royal Purple.

Step 8 — Using a dampened small silk sponge, wipe back the tops of the mountains until the desired color is achieved.

Step 9 — Lightly load a dampened small silk sponge in Mojave Sand and pounce on a clean area of the palette to remove excess color. Lightly sponge color onto the ground areas around the base, being careful to avoid the pueblos.

Step 10 — Repeat Step 8 with Medium Mahogany.

Step 11 — Dip the shader brush in water and touch each side of the brush once to a paper towel to remove excess. Corner load the side of the brush in Sienna Brown and touch once or twice to the palette to work the color through the brush hairs, allowing the color to "float."

With the loaded side of the brush toward the outside, create floated-stroke shading around all pueblo edges.

Step 12 — Using the liner and shader brushes as needed, fill in the uncut windows with Orange.

Step 13 — With the liner brush, add Mahogany Brown dots to the posts near the roof edges of the pueblos.

Step 14 — Using the oval wash mop brush, apply 3 flowing coats of Black Gloss to the sky area. After each coat, clear any excess glaze from the starlight holes with a toothpick.

Step 15 — Fire to cone 6.

Step 16 — Use a rubber-scrubber to smooth the undecorated areas of the fired stoneware surface.

Southwest Plain Indian Vase

DM-1380 Plain Indian Vase Cast with 1 gal. SW 510 Cashmere Stoneware Slip mixed with 4 oz. SW 524 Mocha Stoneware Tint

MATERIALS
CC 111 Dresden Flesh
CC 112 Light Flesh
CC 131 Teal Blue
CC 165 Black
CC 176 Pueblo Purple
CC 177 Santa Fe Sunset
CC 180 Papago Turquoise
HF 583 Black Gloss
SB 803 #4 Liner
TB 715 3/4'' Glaze
TB 736 3/4'' Oval Wash Mop
TL 401 Cleanup or X-acto Knife
TL 415 Replacement Sponge or Large Sea Wool Sponge
Banding Wheel
Soft Lead Pencil
Graphite Paper or Clay Carbon
Rubber-Scrubber

Step 1 — Using the cleanup tool, carefully prepare the greenware. Thoroughly damp-sponge the vase with a large sponge.

Step 2 — Center the vase on a banding wheel and mark a band on top of the flat design surface, 1/4'' in from edge and 1/4'' down side, and another 1/4''-wide band 2'' down from the top edge.

Step 3 — Use the oval wash mop brush loaded with water to dampen the inside of the ware.

Step 4 — Thin Black Gloss to a light cream consistency and roll

inside the vase, being careful not to let glaze drip on the outside of the vase.

Step 5 — Using the glaze brush, apply 3 flowing coats of undiluted Black Gloss to the neck of the vase and the two narrow bands.

Step 6 — Using graphite paper, carefully transfer the pattern with smaller geometrical shapes to the top design area of the vase, making sure the pattern is aligned on both halves of the top. Transfer the pattern with larger geometrical shapes to the sides of the vase between the narrow bands, making cuts in the pattern on the dotted line to allow for the curve of the vase.

Step 7 — Following the numbered patterns as references, use the liner brush to apply 3 smooth, even coats of each Cover-Coat color to the designated areas.

Step 8 — Fire to cone 6.

Step 9 — Use a rubber-scrubber to smooth the undecorated areas of the fired stoneware surface.

PATTERN ON PAGE 38

Contemporary Deep Dish

DM-1060 Deep Dish
Cast with 1 gal SW 520 Cashmere Stoneware Slip mixed with 2 oz. SW 520 Light Taupe Stoneware Tint
and 2 oz. SW 522 Wedgwood Blue Stoneware Tint
(Note: This piece is for decorative purposes only; not for use as dinnerware.)

MATERIALS
HF 583 Black Gloss
SA 885 Teal
AR 951 Sahara Sand
FD 254 Black Licorice
TB 732 #9 Round
TB 736 3/4'' Oval Wash Mop
TL 401 Cleanup or X-acto Knife
TL 415 Replacement Sponge or Large Sea Wool Sponge
Banding Wheel
Soft Lead Pencil
Paper Towels
Rubber-Scrubber

Step 1 — Using the cleanup tool, carefully prepare the greenware.

Step 2 — Damp-sponge the ware with a large sponge to remove any dust.

Step 3 — If desired, use a banding wheel to mark the outer band of the dish. Sketch an off-center wiggly guideline for the French Dimensions.

Step 4 — Thoroughly shake the French Dimensions bottle and squeeze out a small amount on a paper towel to remove any thinned product. Use the #9 round brush to add a line of water over the guideline to ensure product adhesion. Being sure to hold the bottle about $1/8''$ to $1/4''$ above the surface and not in contact with the ware, gently squeeze out Black Licorice on the plate, following the squiggly guideline.

Step 5 — Thoroughly mix crystals in the Sandstar Glaze jar. Using the oval wash mop brush, apply 3 flowing coats of Teal to the smaller half of the design, leaving some space between the glaze and Black Licorice.

Step 6 — Use the oval wash mop brush to apply 3 flowing coats of Sahara Sand to the other half of the design, again leaving space between the glaze and Black Licorice.

Step 7 — With the oval wash mop brush, Apply 3 flowing coats of Black Gloss to the outer band of the dish, applying it within the width of a pencil-point line of the edges of Teal and Sahara Sand (butting glazes).

Step 8 — Fire to cone 6.

Step 9 — Use a rubber-scrubber to smooth the undecorated areas of the fired stoneware surface.

Contemporary Commuter Mug

**DM-1501 Commuter Mug
Cast with 1 gal. SW 510
Cashmere Stoneware Slip
mixed with 4 oz. SW 521
Grey Stoneware Tint**

MATERIALS
EZ 001 Old Rose
EZ 024 Royal Blue Green
EZ 026 Yellow Orange
EZ 027 Navajo Turquoise
EZ 031 Light Blue
EZ 042 Teal
EZ 043 Mint Julep
EZ 046 Apricot Preserves
EZ 051 Santa Fe Sunset
RI 564 Jade Green
HF 577 White Satin
SY 548 Mask 'n Peel
AS 952 Hand and Brush
  Cleaner
SB 805 #8 Shader
TB 715 3/4'' Glaze
TB 731 #7 Round
TL 401 Cleanup or X-acto
  Knife
TL 415 Replacement Sponge
  or Large Sea Wool Sponge
Palette
Rubber-Scrubber

Step 1 — Using the cleanup tool, carefully prepare the greenware. Thoroughly damp-sponge the mug with a large sponge.

Step 2 — Thin Jade Green with water to a light cream consistency and roll inside the mug. Pour out excess, being careful not to get any drips on the outside.

Step 3 — With the glaze brush, apply 3 flowing coats of undiluted Jade Green to the outer lip, about 1'' down, being careful to avoid the handle area.

Step 4 — Condition the round brush in Hand and Brush Cleaner. Use the dampened brush to apply Mask 'n Peel around the lower edge of the handle, and above and below a 2⅝'' band on the flared section of the mug. Allow to dry.

Step 5 — Using the glaze brush, apply 3 flowing coats of White Satin to the flared section of the mug.

Step 6 — Place a small amount of each E-Z Stroke color on separate areas of a palette. If needed, thin the colors to a cream consistency.

Step 7 — Using the shader brush, begin with the brush loaded with Yellow Orange and tipped with Apricot Preserves. Create the flower centers with four to five brushstrokes in random groups around the mug.

Step 8 — Again using the shader brush, create lavender flowers by loading the brush in Santa Fe Sunset and side tipping in Old Rose and Light Blue. Vary the colors on each stroke for interesting shading.

Step 9 — Create blue flowers by loading the shader brush with Light Blue and side tipping with Navajo Turquoise and Teal. Leave some spaces between the flowers for leaves.

Step 10 — Using the shader brush, create leaves by loading the brush with Royal Blue Green tipped with Mint Julep, and randomly pick up a small amount of Yellow Orange, Apricot Preserves and Teal to create variegated leaf colors. Fill in all leaf areas with desired colors.

Step 11 — Carefully remove Mask 'n Peel.

Step 12 — Fire to cone 6.

Step 13 — Use a rubber-scrubber to smooth the undecorated areas of the fired stoneware surface.

Contemporary Extra Large Scalloped Canister

DM-1234 Extra Large Scalloped Canister
DM-1239 Lid for DM-1234
DM-1240 Canister Knob
Cast with SW 510 Cashmere Stoneware Slip

(Note: For a complete Scalloped Canister, you'll need stoneware greenware cast from DM-1235 Large Canister, DM-1236 Medium Canister, DM-1237 Small Canister, DM-1238 Lids for DM-1236 & DM-1237, DM-1239 Lids for DM-1234 & DM-1235 and DM-1240 Canister Knobs.)

MATERIALS
CC 104 Princess Yellow
CC 126 Spring Green
CC 133 Turquoise
CC 134 Stardust Blue
CC 138 Wisteria
CC 142 Canary Yellow
CC 147 Delphinium Blue
CC 148 Deep Turquoise
CC 150 Medium Green
CC 152 Peach
CC 161 Blue Green
CC 169 Peaches 'n Cream
CC 176 Pueblo Purple
CC 177 Santa Fe Sunset
CC 178 Pecos Pink
CC 180 Papago Turquoise
HF 579 Primrose Satin
SB 806 #6 Round
TB 736 ³/₄'' Oval Wash Mop
TL 401 Cleanup or X-acto Knife
TL 415 Replacement Sponge or Large Sea Wool Sponge
Stir Stick
Paper Cup
Graph Paper - 6¹/₄'' x 22³/₄''
Pencil
Graphite Paper or Clay Carbon
Ruler
Rubber-Scrubber

Step 1 — Using the cleanup tool, carefully prepare greenware. Thoroughly damp-sponge the canister and lid, inside and out.

Step 2 — Thin Primrose Satin to a light cream consistency. Roll inside the canister and lid. Wipe away any unwanted glaze from rim areas.

Step 3 — Use the oval wash mop brush to apply 3 flowing coats of undiluted Primrose Satin to the upper area only of the lid (avoiding knob), and to the upper scalloped neck and rim of the canister (avoiding flat inner rim).

Step 4 — On graph paper, create a pattern with overlapping squares and rectangles all over the design area. Pencil in the desired Cover-Coat color numbers to work up design. (See example.)

Step 5 — Transfer pattern onto center design area, using graphite paper.

Step 6 — To create transparency illusion, use #6 round brush to carefully apply 3 smooth, even coats of colors in groups as follows.

Group 1:
104 Princess Yellow
169 Peaches 'n Cream
152 Peach
178 Pecos Pink
138 Wisteria

Group 2:
133 Turquoise
180 Papago Turquoise
161 Blue Green

Group 3:
148 Deep Turquoise
161 Blue Green
126 Spring Green
150 Medium Green
142 Canary Yellow

Group 4:
147 Delphinium Blue
134 Stardust Blue
176 Pueblo Purple
138 Wisteria
177 Santa Fe Sunset

Step 8 — Mix four parts Wax Resist and one part alumina hydrate. Use a #5 round brush reserved for this purpose to apply the mixture to the contact areas of the canister and lid.

Step 9 — With the lid in place on the canister, fire to cone 6.

Step 11 — Remove the protective mixture from the canister and lid with a stiff brush.

Step 12 — Use a rubber-scrubber to smooth the undecorated areas of the fired stoneware surface.

PATTERN ON PAGE 39

Helpful Hints and Reminders

- When taking a stoneware serving dish from the freezer, let it come to room temperature before placing it in the oven, conventional or microwave. Treat stoneware as you would Pyrex glassware.

- NEVER use stoneware items decorated with metallic overglazes in a microwave oven.

- Duncan Overglazes can be used on stoneware surfaces that come into contact with food and drink. Be careful to avoid hard scrubbing when washing overglazed ware, because of the possibility of scraping off the thin layer or metal or luster. Although overglazed stoneware will take repeated washings in a dishwasher, the overglaze will eventually wear away.

- Metallic overglazes applied directly to stoneware surfaces rather than a glazed surface will not be shiny but will produce an attractive dull luster.

- For best results, stoneware greenware should be bone-dry before cleaning. If it is damp, you could score the ware while removing the seam line.

- Remember to leave the bottoms of stoneware items free of glaze (dryfooting), so the pieces will not stick to the kiln shelves.

- Stoneware pieces cannot be stilted for kiln firing. Stilts will bend at high temperatures and could pierce and distort the ware.

- When firing pieces with lids, the two pieces must be fired together to prevent warpage and ensure proper fit.

- When firing pieces with lids or covers, the glazed areas *cannot* touch each other. Do not glaze or underglaze any part of the items that will come in contact with one another. A mixture of 4 parts SY 547 Wax Resist and 1 part alumina hydrate should be applied to these contact areas. This mixture helps prevent pieces from fusing together in the high firing.

- Stoneware shrinks 12-13% when fired to cone 6. Choose your greenware accordingly when doing your own stoneware projects and if in doubt, ask your supplier.

- For a finished professional look, use a rubber-scrubber, 100-grit sandpaper or very fine grit cloth and rub in a circular motion until the surface is smooth. Use a rubber scrubber when buffing over partially glazed pieces to avoid scratching the glaze.

PATTERN
Loaf Pan
FROM PAGE 17

PATTERN
Plain Indian Vase
FROM PAGE 27

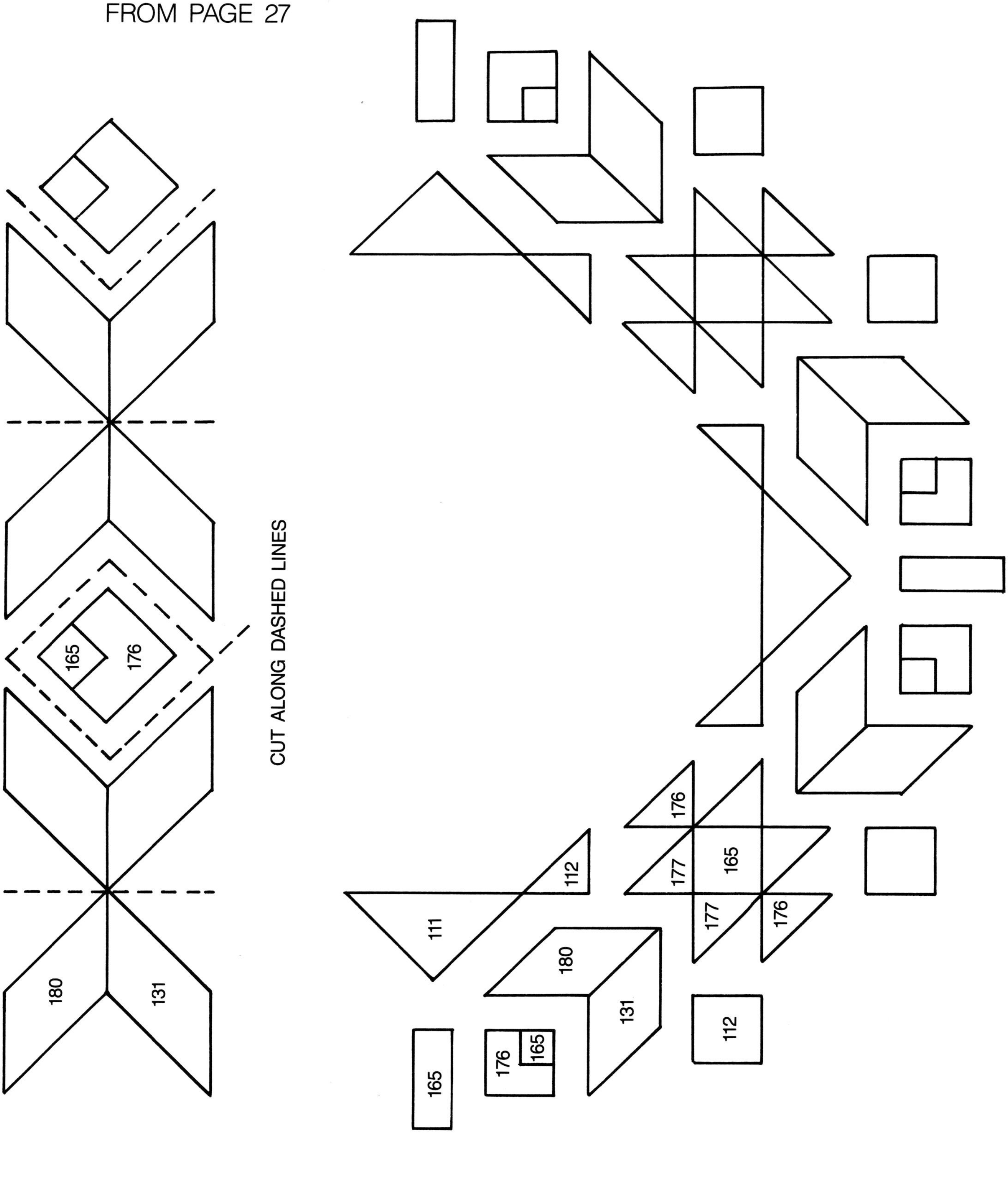

CUT ALONG DASHED LINES

165
176

180
131

111

112

176

177

165

177

176

180

131

112

165

176
165

165

PATTERN
Extra Large
Scalloped Canister
FROM PAGE 33

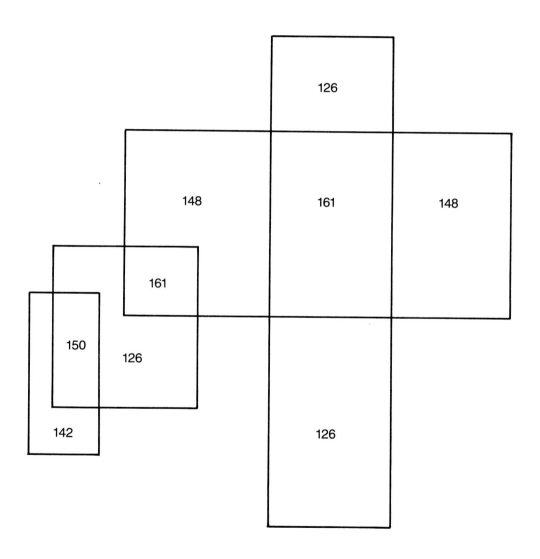

Notes